In this WMG Writer's Guide, *USA Today* bestselling author Dean Wesley Smith takes you step-by-step through Heinlein's Rules and shows how following those rules can change your writing—and career—for the better.

The
WMG Writer's Guide
Series

HEINLEIN'S RULES

FIVE SIMPLE BUSINESS RULES FOR WRITING

A WMG WRITER'S GUIDE

DEAN WESLEY SMITH

wmg PUBLISHING

Heinlein's Rules

Published 2016 by WMG Publishing
www.wmgpublishing.com
Book and cover design copyright © 2016 WMG Publishing
Cover design by Allyson Longueira/WMG Publishing
ISBN-13: 978-1-56146-752-5
ISBN-10: 1-56146-752-9

First published in slightly different form on Dean Wesley Smith's blog
at www.deanwesleysmith.com in 2015

Contents

HEINLEIN'S RULES

FIVE SIMPLE BUSINESS RULES FOR WRITING

A WMG WRITER'S GUIDE

INTRODUCTION

In almost 150 published novels (over one hundred with traditional publishers), I have always followed Heinlein's Business Rules. And in hundreds and hundreds of short stories, I have followed the five rules as well.

For well over thirty years now, actually, I have done my best to stay on Heinlein's Rules. I must admit, I slipped at times, but I'll explain why later on in the book. And how I climbed back on.

So how did I get to these rules? A little about my personal story first.

I started writing at the age of 24 in 1974.

I had hated writing up until that point, but I had to take some English credits to get my degree in architecture, so I took a poetry class for non-majors.

My poems were pretty much hated and the professor called them "commercial." At that point, I had no idea what she was talking about, but it sounded insulting and I was getting a "C" in the class.

Commercial seemed very, very bad.

Then as an assignment, she had her entire class mail a poem to a major national college poetry competition. One of my "commercial" poems won second place and paid me one hundred bucks. The professor had never had a student even get into the book, let alone win.

And I had just made more money than she had total with all of her poetry sales.

Oh, oh... To say I was not popular in the English Department would be an understatement.

But I found writing poems fun and started mailing them out and selling them to top literary journals around the country. Great fun. Seemed major literary magazines liked commercial.

Sold around fifty or so in one year.

And along the way, I thought it would be a lark to write a short story.

So on my trusty electric typewriter, I banged out a 1,000-word story, and didn't rewrite it, just sent it to a horror semi-pro magazine.

They bought it.

I did it again.

They bought the second one.

Spring of 1975 was when things went really wrong. I figured since I was having fun with writing stories, I should learn more about how to write stories, even though I had sold my first two.

So down I went into the myths of writing. (Add bubbling sounds of a person going underwater for the last time.)

I heard I needed to rewrite at least three or four times, so I did, even though I hated to type.

I heard I had to write slow to make it good, so I did, producing exactly two short stories a year for the next seven years.

And every story I thought was gold, a perfect masterpiece of fine art.

All of them were form rejected. And I made it worse by sending each story out only once or twice.

I was convinced the editors were too stupid to see my brilliance.

The two stories I had not touched or rewritten and wrote fast had sold, but the reality was I was too stupid to understand that. I believed in the myths and would defend them, by golly.

But after seven years, by the fall of 1981, I was very, very discouraged. I started looking around at how the writers I admired did what they did.

Bradbury, Silverberg, Ellison, all wrote fast, one draft, and never rewrote past a few minor corrections. And I studied the old pulp writers I admired. Same thing. And I dug through the stories of the literary writers like Hemingway and others. Same thing.

Then by chance, I ran across an edition of *Of Worlds Beyond: The Science of Science Fiction Writing.*

Edited by Lloyd Arthur Eshbach, published in 1947, the book had articles in it by John Taine, Jack Williamson, A.E. van Vogt, L. Sprague de Camp, E. E. "Doc" Smith, John W. Campbell, Jr., and Robert A. Heinlein.

All of the articles are forgettable, sadly, including Heinlein's article, except for the last four paragraphs.

He starts the last four paragraphs with this:

"I'm told that these articles are supposed to be some use to the reader. I have a guilty feeling that all of the above may have been more for my amusement than for your edification. Therefore I shall chuck in as a bonus a group of practical, tested rules, which, if followed meticulously, will prove rewarding to any writer."

Then in one more paragraph he lists his "Business Habits."

1. You must write.

2. You must finish what you start.

3. You must refrain from rewriting except to editorial order.

4. You must put it on the market.

5. You must keep it on the market until sold.

Then Heinlein said this:

"The above five rules really have more to do with how to write speculative fiction than anything said above them. But they are amazingly hard to follow—which is why there are so few professional writers and so many aspirants, and which is why I am not afraid to give away the racket! ..."

I finally understood completely what I had been doing wrong for seven long years. And why my first two stories had sold.

Duh.

So on January 1st, 1982, I made a resolution to write a story per week, following Heinlein's Rules, and mail the story and keep it in the mail.

I wrote 44 stories that first year and started selling regularly in early 1983 and have never looked back.

And stayed focused on those five rules to this day.

Why So Difficult?

The reason these rules are so hard is that they fly into the face, solidly, of what every English teacher on the planet teaches. And has taught from even before Heinlein wrote the rules down.

But remember, English teachers are there to do the almost impossible job of helping students gather knowledge about the language.

They are not there to help a student become a professional fiction writer.

So these simple five business rules smash right into all that learning and teaching we all had as regular English students.

And with the modern world of computers, rewriting is easy, much easier, let me tell you, than it was on a typewriter. So not doing it is even more difficult.

Also, these five rules smash into so many writing myths, it will take most of this book to just detail out how each rule will cause many people to be uncomfortable.

Or even angry.

If one of these rules makes you angry, you need to check in with yourself. Your critical voice is really, really having issues and trying to stop you.

So over the course of this book, I'm going to work through each of the five rules, explaining why the rule is important to becoming a professional fiction writer, how missing a rule stops millions of writers, and how to use the rule in this modern world to access your creative voice and bring fun into your fiction writing.

One note: This is a book about fiction writing. This book is designed to help you on the road to being a professional fiction writer. This does not apply to nonfiction writers or writers of critical essays and the like.

Heinlein was talking about fiction writing. Please keep that clearly in mind.

In 1947, Robert A. Heinlein "…gave away the racket!"

But also, as he said, almost no one can follow these five business rules.

I hope to help you become one of the few who can.

And thus have a long fiction-writing career and fun with your writing.

CHAPTER ONE

For lack of a better way of putting it, Heinlein's Rules allow you to get to the fun of being a writer.

They also help us all remember we are entertainers.

About a decade or so ago, I was asked by a professor of English at the University of Oregon to come talk to one of his advanced creative writing classes about the reality of being a full-time fiction writer.

I had a hunch I was going to not do nice things to their brains. And I looked on that possibility as my sacred job description.

But it turned out I was the one shocked. Before I even had a chance to start to tell them about the fun of writing, about making a living, about writing *Star Trek* or *Men in Black*, one of the students said basically, Mr. Smith, did you know you put such-and-such theme in your story?

I could barely remember the story he was asking about, and I had zero idea that theme was even in there. I know for a fact I didn't layer that in on purpose.

As I sort of sat there facing them, three of them got into an argument about what one of my stories really meant. The poor professor had to stop them to let me talk.

I had no clue any of the stuff they were talking about was even in the story.

Clearly it was, but their attitude about it and how important that was to them shocked me down to my little toes, let me tell you.

I'm an entertainer.

It never occurs to me to add that literary stuff in purposely. But clearly it is there.

Kris had a similar experience back in the Midwest with a college class.

And then another time I got this same lesson is a different way. About twenty years ago, Kris and I were walking along and I asked her which magazine she thought a story I had finished the night before should go.

She suggested a market and then said, "It's one of your wonderful prison stories."

"I don't write prison stories," I said.

I think it took her ten minutes to stop laughing.

It seems, after she explained it to me, that all of my stories, in one fashion or another, are about real people being trapped in some form or another.

Could have fooled me.

I just write to entertain myself.

I guess I have some issues that are deep-seated (or deep-seeded which makes more sense in this case) about being trapped.

But it clearly seems that when I get out of my own way with my writing, my subconscious layers in all sorts of deep and meaningful stuff I don't even think about.

8

Go figure.

And, of course, that's how it has always been with writers.

We write to entertain. It is up to others to figure out what we wrote.

And Heinlein's five business rules help us get to the point where we are just writing and letting the art stuff happen.

Would I have ever gotten to that point of putting that cool stuff (without knowing) in my stories without Heinlein's Rules?

Nope.

Would I have made a living with my fiction for the last numbers of decades without Heinlein's Rules?

Nope.

Would I be enjoying writing as much as I do without Heinlein's Rules?

Not a chance.

Here is My Attitude in Clear Form

—I never look back. I am always focused on the story and then the next story.

—Others can look back for me, either as readers or in some university class. I don't care.

—I write to entertain, first myself, then readers. That is my focus.

—I write because it's the most fun I can have at this age. (No jokes please.)

I think that understanding my attitude will help all readers of this book color how I look at these five simple rules.

One Thing Heinlein's Rules Does Not Talk About

Heinlein's Rules say nothing about typing fast.

They say nothing about speed or anything associated with being prolific.

So many people think they do, but they do not.

For some reason this gets confused and mixed into the rules, but please, if you catch yourself thinking about speed or productivity in association with these five rules, stop and step back.

Heinlein's Rules are business rules.

So with all that said, onward into the rules.

CHAPTER TWO

*R*ule #1... *You must write.*
How simple.

On the surface, this sounds so easy. Of course, just write. Duh.

Well, how about some reality?

Say you have one million people who say they want to be writers, who have a book in them they really want to write, who have a dream about writing stories and maybe getting published.

One million. There are a lot more than that, of course, but for this example that number is round.

My opinion, of that one million, nine hundred thousand will never find the time.

That's just my rough and more-than-likely conservative guess. But it is a guess on my part from decades of watching.

Nine out of ten people can't find the time to write, even though they say they want to.

Or another way to look at this, in my opinion over 90% of all people who say they would like to write, who say they want to write someday, are wiped out by Heinlein's Rule #1.

Yeah, the first rule sounds so, so, so simple, doesn't it?

You must write.

Period.

Yet it is the most deadly of all the rules.

Writer vs. Author

My definition of a writer is a person who writes.

My definition of an author is a person who has written.

Yeah, I agree, sort of a nasty distinction. I have no respect for authors. I have a ton of respect for writers.

(And right there a massive herd of authors just left this book. Ahhh, well, they had promotion to do, after all.)

In this modern world of indie publishing, we see a ton of authors out there pushing their one or two or three books, promoting them to death, annoying their two hundred Twitter followers and their family on Facebook.

Promotion is not writing. That's just being an author.

Writers are people who write.

Also, Heinlein did not say, *You must research.*

Research is not writing.

Also, Heinlein did not say, *You must promote.*

Promotion of your last novel is not writing.

Talking with your friends in a workshop about your future book is not writing.

Outlining your novel is not writing.

And on and on.

Back to ***Rule #1: You must write.***

So simple.

So hard for so many.

My friend Kevin J. Anderson sent me a wonderful card when I sold my first novel. I sold my first novel about a year ahead of his first novel sale, yet he clearly understood what was going on better than I did at that point.

The card was priceless, and I still have it.

On the front the card was divided into six panels. Each panel showed this mouse sweating to push this huge elephant up a hill. And with each panel the elephant got higher on the hill.

I opened the card and there, inside, was the elephant sitting at the top of the hill and the mouse looking down at a herd of elephants in valley below.

The caption on the card said, "**Congratulations! Now, do it again.**"

Exactly.

Now, almost thirty years later (I sold that first novel in May of 1987) I am still having a great time moving those elephants to the top of the hill, one right after another.

Writers are people who write.

I am a writer.

And thanks to Heinlein's Rules, especially Rule #1, I make my living writing fiction.

And I have since 1987.

CHAPTER THREE

S till working on rule number one.
  Rule #1: You Must Write.

Back in 1982, when I climbed onto my challenge to use Heinlein's Rules and write a story per week and mail each story every week, I had one major issue that I fought.

Fear.

No idea what I was afraid of, but the fear was real.

On December 31st, 1981, my thinking was that every story had to be perfect, had to be worked over and over before I dared send it out. And it had to be written slowly and carefully to be good. I believed everything English teachers taught me.

Hook, line, and sinker.

One day later, January 1st, 1982, I went to Heinlein's Rules, not rewriting, writing a story and just mailing it after fixing typos.

Cold turkey.

So from that moment forward, I thought that every story I sent out was crap. Total crap.

I didn't just think that, I believed it completely.

I had no doubt. None.

I was still in the "must be perfect" mode (kidding myself that I knew what perfect even was, of course).

But I was going to give the Heinlein's Rules challenge a try because so many major writers wrote that way and I had had no luck at all the other way for seven years.

So week after week, I mailed off stories I thought sucked. Oh, I did my best on them, made sure they were as typo-free as possible, but I spent no time on them as I had with my precious two-stories-per-year gems that sat molding in files.

And fairly quickly the form rejections turned to personal letters and then to nice letters from editors. Shock!

Then early in the second year I started selling. I sold to *Writers of the Future, Oui Magazine, Gem Magazine,* and to a Damon Knight edited anthology. (You can still read my story in volume #1 of *Writers of the Future.*)

And the sales kept rolling in.

I still thought every story I wrote was crap.

Every one of them.

But I was starting to catch a clue that if I just let my subconscious tell the story and stay out of its way, my stories were pretty good.

Also, I kept learning and seeking out details of advice that made sense with my new way of approaching things.

What was also happening at writing a story per week was that I was practicing. I wrote more in the first fifteen weeks of 1982 than I did in the previous seven years.

Any wonder my stuff got better?

You Must Write.

I had figured out a way to do that.

Dare to be Bad

One fine day during that first year, I was complaining to the great fantasy writer Nina Kiriki Hoffman about how I felt I was mailing out crap every week. Sure, I was staring to get nice letters from editors, but I still couldn't get past the training of wanting to make every story "perfect."

And I felt like I often wrote stories too quickly, so they couldn't be good.

Yup, even six months or so into the challenge of following Heinlein's Rules, I was still lost in the myths. Completely.

Nina was living above my bookstore and she was doing the same challenge I was. We had bet each other to get a new story per week out.

Now I was in law school, had a job tending bar, and I owned and ran a bookstore. I was married and I had no time to write a story per week, but I was doing it.

Nina was still in college. She had no time either. But she was doing it also.

So in response that day to my complaining about how I felt I was mailing out crap, Nina basically said, "It takes more courage to try something and fail than to not try at all."

We talked about how true that was, and Nina coined the phrase "Dare to be bad."

It takes more courage to write and put the story out than it does to only talk about writing and not do it. You have to dare to fail sometimes.

So I took that saying and stenciled it in big letters and tacked it on the wall over my typewriter in my bookstore.

Dare to be bad.

What that saying did to help me seemed critical in one area. That saying got me past the fear of writing.

Rule #1: You Must Write.

What stops most people isn't lack of time, it's fear.

Committing words to paper means you might have to show them to someone. The words might fail; you might be found wanting.

So it is easier to let the fear stop you before you even get to Rule #1.

Most people who say they would like to write are just too afraid and don't know how to get past the fear.

The "Dare to be Bad" saying helped me jump past the fear.

And what that ultimately did was allow my subconscious to do the work.

My job became, fairly quickly, staying out of the way of my subconscious and just mailing the final product, no matter what my conscious brain thought of it.

That's right. I have trained my critical front brain to just stay out of the way of the storyteller that is my back brain.

Easier said than done, and still a constant fight.

To this day, when I hand a story or a novel to Kris, I believe it is crap. I have learned my critical judgment means nothing when it comes to my own work.

And when Kris hands me something she wrote and says it sucks, I know I am in for a real treat.

Why?

Because if Kris's critical brain is afraid of something she wrote, that means she took chances, went to places she had never been before, took risks with the story or the writing.

And she knows that even if she thinks the story sucks, she needs to release it to someone who has perspective.

Kris won a Hugo Award for her editing, and yet with her own work, she can't judge it.

No writer can.

So does that mean the fear isn't real that we all feel?

Nope. It's a real fear.

Trust me, I feel it with every story or novel I finish.

But the only repercussion on the negative side is that you allow the fear to win. If you release the story, you quickly come to see that the fear is baseless.

Doesn't make it feel any less real, however.

And it is this fear of some made-up repercussion that stops most of the 90% of writers who say they want to write and can't find the time.

Anyone can find the time to write a little every day.

But only about 1 in 10 can figure out a way, as I did, to climb past the fear, or just live with the fear of failure by writing.

It is better to write and fail then not write at all.

Rule #1. You must write.

Dare to be Bad.

You might discover along the way just how good a storyteller your subconscious really is.

I did.

CHAPTER FOUR

M oving now to the second rule.
    Rule #2: You Must Finish What You Write.

Say 9 out of 10 people who claim they want to write are wiped out by Rule #1 because they "just can't find the time."

If that is the case, then my guess is that another half of the remaining writers are stopped cold by Rule #2.

Now, I have to be honest, I never had an issue with this rule, so I mostly just ignored it. I always finished what I wrote. Part of that was the early challenge to mail a story per week, but mostly I just hate leaving things unfinished.

So until Kris and I started teaching workshops, I had no idea how really deadly this not-finishing-projects was to many, many writers. I just had no idea, because it is not my problem.

So I talked with a lot of writers over the last fifteen years about various aspects of this problem of not finishing.

And I started watching all the excuses people give for not finishing, and it became clear how really deadly this rule is for many.

At first I thought it was a craft problem writers had. I thought maybe writers didn't understand the ending structure, or how to build to an end, or even how to see an ending.

Sure, there were minor aspects of that, but when that was scraped away, it boiled down to a few common problems I'll detail below.

How it Works

The feeling of this problem goes like this for many:

Step one: Excitement about a story or an idea.

Step two: Excitement carries the writer a distance into the story or novel or an outline.

Step three: Excitement wears off, critical voice plows in, story looks like crap and too much work to keep going.

Step four: Writer makes up some excuse to stop and go find a project that is exciting again.

Step five: Repeat the first four steps without ever finishing anything.

Outlines do not help this problem.

Finishing has been made into an "important event" and thus almost impossible to actually get to. Like that pot of gold at the end of a rainbow.

As long as you are working on something, you can call yourself a writer. But when you finish, you aren't writing, so it is better to stay a writer and just keep working on it.

You can't fail if you just keep working on a project.

Writers with this problem can't see not finishing as failure.

Two Major Areas

1. Fear

To put it simply, finishing something risks that what you finished will fail.

In my early days, failure was the story not selling to an editor. In this modern world, it can still be that, or it can be that you put it out indie and no one buys it.

If you keep working on something to make it better, rewriting it for the fifth time, reworking that plot you don't think works, and so on and so on, you won't risk the failure of no readers in the end.

To writers with this problem, a story must be some imaginary image of "perfect" before it can be released. And no story ever attains that.

For any of us, actually.

Kris did an entire book on this called "The Pursuit of Perfection." That book deals with this problem and so much more and worth your time and money if you have this problem.

Fear of failure is real and if it has become the dominating force in your writing, you need to go get professional help to get past the problem. It is that serious. Not kidding.

Rule #3 coming up also works into this rule.

Finishing a sloppy first draft that you must rewrite is not finishing. Sorry.

As long as you are working on a story in some fashion or another, it is not finished, and thus you don't have to risk the fear of failure.

And a small slice of writers have this issue because of fear of success. Not kidding here either. They don't finish because their ego tells them their work is so wonderful, it will be an instant bestseller and they don't want to be famous.

I have met a couple of these writers. I managed to not laugh until I walked out of the room.

Also, finishing brings in another fear.

Fear of mailing.

I have been an editor off and on for over thirty years. Not once do I remember a story that didn't work. Why?

Because editors don't read stories that don't work.

Duh.

I can't even remember the thousands of stories I have bought at various magazines over the years, let alone any story I didn't read.

Duh.

But yet the fear of mailing to an editor scares some writers beyond words. So they are better off not finishing than to have to face that fear.

And now the fear of learning how to indie publish scares writers, so better to not finish than have to learn all the new stuff.

Fear.

On and on.

Excuse after excuse.

2. Love of a Project

This is also fear-based, but in a different way. It goes like this: "If I finish this project, what do I do next?"

This boils down to the early fear all writers have of not finding another idea. I do a six-week online workshop called "Ideas to Story" that helps writers fix that issue completely.

And as you write more and more, you quickly come to realize that ideas are everywhere and far too many for you to ever get to.

I used to write ideas down in notebooks because of this fear. But after a few years I stopped because if I couldn't remember the idea in a week, it wouldn't be worth my time to write it.

And now I never even come up with ideas.

I don't. Honest.

I write from triggers, an advanced way of telling stories, granted. But given enough time, every writer can get there.

But I do understand this excuse to not finish. I have a number of worlds I love to play inside. But I write and finish stories and novels inside the worlds. I never just work on one thing for years.

But I have seen more writers than I want to admit that are working on "their novel." When they say that, you know this is their problem and Rule #2 is going to kill them.

Writers like this will finish a draft, maybe, then go into major rewrites, even though they have no idea how to rewrite or how to tell a better story, they still need to stir the words around.

Then they give it to some "editor" that they pay a vast amount of money to (called a scam) and the editor has them work on it some more.

And on and on.

Never finishing.

Sadly, I have never seen a writer find a solution to this. They can't even admit the problem to themselves so they just cycle in the same world, same characters.

These writers will never finish because if they finished, all the people around them who had watched them work on "their novel" for years might actually have a chance to read it.

Far, far too dangerous to allow to happen.

You also see this with most of the sloppily drafted NaNoWriMo novels. They will never be fixed and no one will ever read them because it's too dangerous for the writer to let their supportive family who sacrificed time so they could write see how really bad the book might be.

If Writing Is Not Fun

Writers who can't seem to finish much, if anything, believe in the tortured "artist" myth, that writing must be hard and only years of working in the salt mines can make a novel brilliant.

Nope. That's a myth.

Thankfully.

So two major reasons why this simple Rule #2 stops so many writers.

1. Fear of failure.

2. Fear of moving on to something new.

Notice fear is the major word in both.

If a fear of any kind is crippling you and stopping you from finishing a novel or story, don't fight the story through. You won't beat the fear that way.

Step outside of that one novel, that one story, and deal with the fear outside of any one story.

What are you afraid will happen?

And is that worse than never finishing anything?

Heinlein's Rules are so simple. Remember, even he said that.

So let me lay out clearly what he meant with the first two rules in relationship to failure and fear of failure.

Think of the rules this way:

Rule #1… You Must Write. Not writing is failure.

Rule #2… You Must Finish What You Write. Not finishing is failure.

So if you are having fear issues, move the fear over to not writing and not finishing.

I can tell you this for a fact: The idea of not writing and not finishing what I write scares hell out of me.

Get help with your fears, move the fear to a fear of not writing.

And move the fear to a fear of not finishing.

Because not writing and not finishing are true failures.

I hate to tell you this folks: Every time you claim you want to write and then don't write or don't finish, everyone around you knows you are failing.

That should scare you more than anything.

CHAPTER FIVE

Moving now to the third rule.
Rule #3: You Must Refrain from Rewriting Unless to Editorial Order.

So, this is the rule that gets all the attention here in the modern world, even though it is the first two rules that stop most wannabe writers. And the fourth rule also stops writers who can finish something from becoming professional writers.

Everybody in this modern world looks for ways and reasons around this rule. That's how ingrained the modern myth of rewriting is in our culture.

One good thing right off about this rule: If you don't rewrite, just get it correct the first time through, you have more time to write new stories. And writers are always pressed for time.

Yet, time seems to make no difference to writers having trouble with this rule.

Rule #3 is actually an offshoot of Rule #2 failure.

Rule #2 is that you must finish what you write. If you are re-writing, you are not finishing.

And this rule plays right smack into every beginning writer's fear that what they wrote isn't good enough.

(Personally, I'm not sure where the thinking comes from that if they couldn't get it correct the first time, why looking at it and stirring the words around will make it better, but that is the myth.)

So there is a lot to this rule.

And people are always wondering what Heinlein really meant.

Well, he meant exactly what he wrote. You must refrain from rewriting unless to editorial order.

Period.

That simple.

So let me break the rule down into the three parts and try to show how some of these parts work and why they fit just fine in the modern world if you actually follow the rule as Heinlein intended.

Part One… You Must Refrain

Part Two… Rewriting

Part Three… Unless to Editorial Order

Part One of Rule #3… You Must Refrain

Heinlein, at the time he wrote this, was talking to beginning writers about what they were hearing about writing. At the time, in 1947, university programs were booming because of the GI Bill and so many WWII vets going back to school.

English teachers by this point in time had bought completely into the articles published in the late 1800s about how writing slowly would make better literature.

And at the same time writers such as Hemingway were tired of all the new-writer questions as being stupid. Everyone knew Hemingway was a reporter who wrote one-draft fast articles and books. He had made that clear.

Yet he still kept getting the same questions, as all experienced writers get, from wave after wave of new writers. So he started making stuff up about how he wrote, making it so outlandish that he was sure that writers would just laugh and realize they were being made fun of.

Of course, new writers have no sense of humor, so generations of new writers wrote standing up and did thirty or forty drafts because Hemingway told them to. It was a joke, folks.

So when Heinlein wrote his article and gave his five business rules, he was in a way trying to tell the truth to young writers to fight the idiocy coming out of Hemingway's jokes.

So the phrase "You must refrain..." means exactly that. Do not think about a second draft. Just flat don't do them.

Get it right the first time through. Just refrain from what some writers were saying in jokes and English teachers were spreading around to get writers to slow down so they didn't have to read as much.

Also, at the point Heinlein wrote this, the pulp magazines and digests were still going strong and building circulation again after the war. Writers wrote for 1 cent per word on typewriters. As one major pulp writer said when asked, "They don't pay me to rewrite."

Part Two of Rule #3... Rewriting

What is rewriting? Wow, can't tell you how often I get that question and writers want me to define it right down to how much they can and can't touch.

Well, first let me tell you what rewriting is not. Got that?

Rewriting is not:
—Fixing errors
—Fixing typos
—Fixing wrong details

If you want to know how Heinlein and other major one-draft writers used to do it, simply find online some of their pages of manuscripts. I am sure the pages put online will be the most marked up, but that's fine as well.

What those of us who started with typewriters knew was that you could fix mistakes on a page before mailing it. Up to ten mistakes before you had to retype the page. That's why the manuscript format is double spaced, so there is room between lines to add in words or even a sentence.

Most of Heinlein's manuscripts have a hand correction about every page of a detail fixed. At least the manuscripts I have seen.

I've also seen a lot of Harlan Ellison manuscripts. You know he wrote one draft on a typewriter in store windows and posted each page as he finished it. I was also his publisher for a time and his manuscripts are very clean, usually only one or two word corrections a page.

You get the story correct the first time, but you can fix typos, spelling, and wrong details.

That's what Heinlein meant.

That's what I mean.

It really is that simple.

Creative vs. Critical Voice

Over the years I have spent a lot of time talking about the difference between writing in creative voice and writing in critical voice.

Critical voice is that voice in your head that says everything is shit. That your story is bad, that you must fix it.

That's critical voice. Nothing good ever comes from critical voice. Critical voice wants to make your stuff the same and safe and dull.

Creative voice is that surprising place where nifty stuff just springs forth.

Professional writers have learned to leave that creative voice alone and let it work. We do everything in our power to stay out of its way and then not change what it has produced (other than fixing typos and small details.)

—Rewriting comes from the thought, "I need to fix that before it goes out."

That's critical voice and it is almost always wrong. When you hear that, just fix the typos and mail the story or publish it and move on.

—Rewriting is also caused by sloppy first drafts. Somewhere over the last twenty or thirty years, a deadly saying has cropped up. "Get it down, then fix it."

This makes writing from creative voice almost impossible.

Think of your creative voice as a two-year-old kid. If you tell that voice that it can do what it wants, but it won't matter, parents (critical voice) will just make it better later, the kid won't want to play at all.

But if you follow Heinlein's 3rd rule and promise your creative voice you won't touch what the creative voice comes up with, you will be amazed at how freeing that is and how much original and unique work comes out.

The idea of sloppy writing is just such a waste of time.

Basically, when Heinlein said, "You must refrain from rewriting…" he was telling new writers to work to get it right the first time through.

Yeah, yeah, I know, that's not what your English teacher told you. That's not the myth.

So keep doing many, many drafts, maybe as many as Hemingway told you to do, and remain an aspirant as Heinlein said.

Also remember, if you are rewriting things all the time, you are not finishing anything and Rule #2 has got you in its grips.

Part Three of Rule #3… Unless to Editorial Order

This used to be such a forgotten part of this rule for decades. It was obvious.

If you mailed off your story or novel to a major editor and the editor asked for a rewrite to fix something to help the story fit their magazine or book line better, then you considered it.

You might do it, you might decline.

Harlan Ellison added to Heinlein's rule… "And then only if you agree."

All of that still applies.

But this new world has really confused things for this last little clause of rule #3.

First off, agents are not editors.

Duh.

Yet beginning writers will rewrite and rewrite and rewrite for agents who can't write a check or even have a clue what they are doing.

I'll be honest, and I have talked about it number of times on my blog, this practice is the stupidest thing I have ever seen in publishing.

Period.

If you are trapped in such stupidity, here is my suggestion:

Stop!!!

Withdraw the book and move on. Go back to your first original draft and trust your own writing and voice. Act like an artist instead of a doormat for heaven's sake.

Second, some scam book doctors you pay are not editors.

If you pay someone, they are NOT AN EDITOR. They can't write you a check. In fact, you are paying them so you can be scammed and your book ruined.

Unless this editor has published fifty or more novels, just STOP!!!

Withdraw the book, count the money spent as learning, and start trusting your own voice and writing. Again, act like an artist.

Again, the only exception to this is if the book-doctor/editor is a major published writer and knows what they are talking about.

But most writers go to "editors" who have published a couple how-to-write scam books.

Seriously?

Think, people, just think.

So what to do with Heinlein's Rule #3?

Follow it.

Completely.

Write the best story or book you can the first time through.

Fix typos and spelling mistakes.

Give the book to a trusted first reader, then fix the nits they find.

Then move on to rule #4.

Yup, that simple.

And really, really that hard in this world of rewriting myths.

As Heinlein said, these rules look simple and are almost impossible to follow.

Why are they impossible to follow? Because simply, you won't let yourself follow them.

You are the only person stopping yourself.

And think about how much more fun you'll have writing if you don't rewrite.

And how much more time you'll have to play with new stories.

CHAPTER SIX

Continuing with the third rule.
Rule #3: You Must Refrain from Rewriting Unless to Editorial Order.

I wanted to go at this rule one more time to make sure I've been clear. Most of the time, in this modern world, rewriting is when you do a sloppy first draft with the intent of "letting it sit" (dumbest thing I have ever heard) and then "fix it" later.

That assumes, of course, that your story is broken.

And that you have suddenly gained a vast amount of new skills since doing the story the first time.

I will often get comments from writers in workshops when I say, "Great job. It works fine." The writer wants to know what is wrong. If I don't say anything is wrong, nothing is wrong.

That kind of thinking, of always thinking something is broken, comes directly out of this myth that everything must be rewritten because it is clearly broken.

If you tell your creative voice to do it right the first time, the story won't be broken.

It might not work the way you feel it should, but it won't be broken and some readers might think it works just fine as is.

Cycling

This modern world of computers has allowed us to use a wonderful new method of writing fiction. That's called cycling.

The first thing you must understand about this new method of working in creative voice to create a clean story the first time through is that you, the author, are the god of your story.

You are unstuck in time in your story.

You could write the last line, the first line, a middle line, and then jump around filling in gaps.

The intent is to make a story that the reader will start into on page one, word one, and end up at the last word.

BUT YOU DON'T HAVE TO WRITE IT THAT WAY.

This is the hardest concept for a new writer to grasp after English classes. English teachers talk about the complexity and all that of fiction, and all of us thought that the authors must have been really brilliant to start from that first word and put all that nifty stuff in at exactly the right moment.

Nope.

You are the god of your own story, you can jump around all you want in your story and do anything you want.

As long as you do it in creative mode.

In the old days, writers would add in pages, or hand-write in sentences in earlier pages that needed to be added because of something that came later in the story.

I would often have a page that was numbered 3a that came right after page 3 in my story.

In our modern world of computers, we can cycle back in creative mode and just add in or take out what we want when we want.

How I do it (and it turns out, many other professionals I have talked to are the same) is that I write about 400 to 600 words (into the dark) and then bog down.

I instantly jump back to the start of those 400 words and run through them, adding in a detail, reading it, touching it, until I am back to the blank page with some speed and I go another 400 to 600 words. Then I cycle back about 500 words and do it again.

If you graphed it, it would look like I am moving forward and then jumping up out of the timeline and circling back into the timeline of the story and then going forward again.

I'll repeat until I get to the end and the story is done and clean because I have looked at most of it twice. (I talk a lot more about this method in the book *Writing into the Dark.*)

I do this all while my creative voice is in control.

I average about 1,000 words per hour of finished story with this method, which always includes a five-minute break every hour.

Rewriting has been made easy with computers. That is the huge problem.

But cycling isn't rewriting, it's just using the computer tool to do what writers have always done. Jump around in time in our stories.

So remember, just because the reader will read a story from word one to the final word doesn't mean you have to write it that way.

Editors

Let me describe the types of editors there are in this new world just to be very clear.

Traditional Editor

This editor is hired by a magazine or a book company to put together a magazine or a book line. They have very specific things they are looking for and will often ask you to touch up your book, do a pass through the book to help it fit their book line or magazine better.

That's the kind of thing Heinlein was talking about with the last part of Rule #3. **These editors can write you checks for your work.**

Book Doctors/Developmental Editors/Content Editors

All of these types of editors you pay are scams. (With the exceptions of major writers with long careers helping out younger writers for a fee.)

Granted, many of these book doctors have their hearts in the right place. I understand that. They want to help young writers, but the book doctors (or developmental editors or whatever you call them) have no credentials and could no more tell what makes a better book than your neighbor down the street. (Actually, feedback from your neighbor might be better.)

So they are actually hurting young writers instead of helping them.

Do not pay these book doctors. Just trust your own creative voice, your own art.

And focus on learning how to tell better stories over years by how-to books, taking classes, and listening to writers who have forty or fifty novels published.

In other words, learn from those a ways down the road that you want to walk and never grovel and pay someone with no credentials.

Line Editors

Line editors are editors who look for consistency in your story and your words. They look for clarity. Great line editors are extremely rare and most writers can get by without them.

Often great line editors are also buying editors for magazines or anthologies. John Helfers is a great line editor and he often buys for anthologies and edits a volume of *Fiction River* for WMG Publishing every year.

Copyeditors

Every indie writer needs to hire a copyeditor. You can find them in services and locally from newspapers and such. Copyeditors look for nits, mistakes, wrong words spelled correctly.

Great copyeditors are priceless as well, but you must, as an indie writer, hire one. No manuscript should go into print without a good copyeditor looking at it.

I am posting this book on my blog in rough form. It will be run through a copyeditor before it sees electronic and paper print.

Copyediting is not rewriting. Copyediting is simply finding the last wave of mistakes and cleaning as many of then out as they can find.

But no book is perfect. None.

We all do the best we can and release and move on.

Summary of Rule #3

Heinlein was basically trying to help writers learn how to write a story, do the best they could, release and move on.

Forward.

Always face forward.

Think of your writing journey as a walking trip. When you write a story, you are walking forward, helping yourself by learning and practicing and creating more stories that might sell and get you readers.

But the moment you stop and turn around to rewrite something, you have stopped your forward momentum and actually walked backwards to hurt your fiction.

Forward.

Always face and move forward.

The modern world has developed this fantastically powerful myth that all writing must be rewritten to be good. And no writer coming into fiction writing is immune from the pressure of the myth.

Writing is an art.

Good stories come from the creative side of our minds. To tell good stories, you must train that creative side to let go and play.

Write the story, finish the story, release the story. Rules 1-3.

It really is as simple as Heinlein said.

But in this modern world, it is really that hard.

CHAPTER SEVEN

On to the fourth rule.

Rule #4: You Must Put It on the Market.

"It" in the rule refers to your finished and not rewritten story or novel.

On the surface, this rule is very, very basic. And yet it was this rule that I had the most problem with over the years.

This and Rule #5.

Old Traditional Publishing World

What Heinlein meant when he wrote this business rule in 1947 was that you had to send your story to some market that would buy it, publish it, and pay you money.

When I started with these rules in 1982, the meaning was exactly the same. So I started off writing, finishing, and mailing a short story every week to a magazine or anthology that might buy it. I did the writing on an electric typewriter and I didn't rewrite. (I did fix typos.)

I did 44 stories that first year, 43 the second year, (while working three jobs) and was selling regularly by the end of the start of the second year. In fact, by the end of the second year, I had 16 short-story sales.

This was all fine and swell and nifty as long as I was only writing short stories. But then I started writing novels.

I still wrote short stories following Heinlein's Rules, but I would often just show them to Kris and then never get around to mailing them.

Over the years, knowing I had this problem, I started a number of things that were designed to help me follow this rule.

One solution was called "The Race."

The Race was simple. You got one point for every short story you had in the mail to a market (remember, this is pre-indie world), three points for every chapter and outline you had out, and eight points for every full novel you had under submission.

I managed just over 70 different short stories in the mail at the same time during the years the race was going on in my writer magazine called *The Report*.

I was not leading the race.

Kevin J. Anderson and Kristine Kathryn Rusch were always ahead of me in points.

It is amazing, looking back at those old issues of *The Report* from the late 1980s that the names that were on the top of The Race ended up with long careers and the names with only had a few stories out in the race aren't around anymore.

Heinlein said, "You must put it on the market."

But chances are the writers at the bottom of The Race during those years had issues with the first three rules. Kevin, Kris, and I had no issue with those first three. And The Race was a fun way to help us all keep stuff out.

Actually, it helped me.

42

But to this day, I still find stories that I never mailed.

Wonder why I never sold the stories, huh?

But for the most part, I managed to keep on Rule #4.

The New World of Publishing

Wow, do authors today have more choices for their stories and novels than Heinlein did in 1947.

Or what I did in 1982.

A ton more.

But the meaning of Rule #4 remains solid.

When you finish a story or novel, you must put it on the market.

But what does "market" mean in this modern world?

Well, for short fiction, the traditional rules still work fine. In fact, this is a new golden age for short fiction with as many magazines publishing fiction now as in the 1940s.

So mailing short stories to traditional magazines like I did in the 1980s and 1990s still works great. And I recommend it with short fiction.

As far as mailing novels into the traditional publishing world, I DO NOT recommend it at the moment. Contracts are very bad, advances are so low as to be laughable, and it flat takes too long for anything to get to readers who have grown used to getting it Now!

What to know an interesting bit about Heinlein in his day. Novels were mostly sold to pulp magazines. And ended up in books later, if they were lucky.

When I started writing and mailing novels in the mid-1980s, you sent your work directly to book editors and often sold the editors projects over lunch at conventions.

Those days, both Heinlein's and my early days, are long gone.

For now, stay away from traditional book publishers and their lackey agents. You will be glad you did.

Sending a book to an agent IS NOT PUTTING IT ON THE MARKET.

Sorry. Agents can't write you a check for your work.

Agents are not a market.

Indie Publishing

The new world of indie publishing has exploded since 2009. Now a writer, with some learning, can get a book copyedited and to readers within a month or so from finishing it.

Writers now deal directly with readers.

Getting a book or story out for sale to readers is putting it on the market.

In fact, that is the clear, bottom line of the word "market." Readers are the end product of all storytelling.

Readers are the market.

So Rule #4 now has many, many choices for writers. And that's a good thing. Stressful at times, sure, but a good thing.

For example, in July of 2015, I decided to write a short story per day. It was great fun and I actually did 32 short stories in 31 days.

I followed Heinlein's first three rules to the letter.

But what was I going to do for Rule #4 with those 32 short stories?

First off, I put them all together, plus the blog each night about the process of writing the stories, did a cover for each story, a blurb for each story, and put them all in a book called *Stories from July* that came out just two months after I finished the last story.

So in two months all the short stories were all on the market.

I will be, in 2016, putting some of those stories into my magazine called *Smith's Monthly*. (I usually have four or five stories per issue every month.)

A second market for many of the stories I wrote in July.

I will also be putting many of the stories in short-story collections over the next few years.

A third market for many of them.

And each story will be for sale in 2016 as a standalone story for readers to buy.

A fourth market for all of them.

For a person who has had a lot of trouble over the decades with Rule #4, I'm pretty proud of what I am doing now when it comes to this rule. I think I have finally managed, after over three decades, to wrestle this simple-sounding rule to the ground.

Finally.

Must Talk About Fear

Now, this is a problem area I have observed when it comes to this rule. And I know it is real.

But I have no deep understanding of the problem. My reason for not mailing a story was just laziness or lack of organization or a bad memory that I had even written the story.

But for some reason, many writers are flat afraid to mail their work to editors or indie publish their work.

I guess writers feel that the editor or reader might hate their work and do some sort of mortal damage to the writer.

I guess.

Damned if I know. Just seems really silly to me.

So, let me tell you the reality, folks.

Readers (not jerky critics) don't read or buy something they don't like.

Editors don't read or buy something that doesn't fit what they are looking for.

Over my decades of editing, I can't begin to remember the stories I have bought, which means I loved them and worked with the author and paid the author money.

Why would any author think an editor who only glances at a story, knows it won't work, and passes on it, will remember the author?

Or the story?

Ego. Wow.

I think this fear might come from "my manuscript is my baby" problem some writers have. And of course, every editor's desk is empty, just waiting for the writer's baby to appear in front of the editor so the editor can take their time reading it and remembering every blessed word.

Ego.

But editors don't work that way.

And neither do readers. Even if your wonderful cover catches them, your perfect, active blurb draws them in, if the opening of your book or story doesn't work, the reader will move on and not buy it or read it.

And they won't remember the writer.

Readers are the ultimate editors.

So this fear of mailing is just damn silly on the face and under the surface.

Get over it.

Get over yourself.

Follow the fourth rule.

Summary of Rule #4

"You must put it (your story or novel) on the market."

Very simple, yet scary hard for many to do.

My only suggestion is to figure out systems that work for you to get the story from your computer and on the way to a magazine editor or a reader who can buy it.

And if your system breaks down, change it, fix it, get the stories out there.

Get past the fear, get past your ego, and just do it.

Rule #1 stops a vast majority of people who dream of writing.

Rule #2 stops a vast majority of the people who make it past Rule #1.

Rule #3 destroys stories and sends the writers back into Rule #2 problems.

Rule #4 stops careers of a vast majority of the writers who did make it past the first three rules.

And in the next chapter, Rule #5 wipes out even more.

As Heinlein said, these are simple rules. Deadly if not followed, but simple to understand.

CHAPTER EIGHT

O n to the fifth rule.

Rule #5: You Must Keep It on the Market Until Sold.

"It" in the rule refers to your story or novel.

In 1947, when Heinlein wrote this rule, for the most part the only markets were pulp magazines. Paperbacks were just gaining strength and hardback publishers were very, very selective.

So all short stories and most novels were sold to pulp magazines, and the few digest magazines that were starting up, and maybe to the slick magazines such as *Saturday Evening Post*, if you were good and well-known as a writer.

But as with today, there were enough markets in 1947 to make this fifth rule a great business rule.

There are a million stories over the decades of how many times some book or story was rejected before being bought.

I had one story rejected over thirty times before finally selling it to a top market I had never thought of before.

I was following Heinlein's Rules.

Indie Publishing

The new world of indie publishing causes this rule to change slightly to follow Heinlein's intent.

If you put a story up for sale indie, the rule basically means leave it there.

I have heard of so many writers who, for some reason unknown to my way of thinking, gave up on a story or novel because it didn't sell to some preconceived level and pulled the story down.

And never put the story or novel back up.

In the old traditional days, we used to have a saying: "No story sold while sitting in your top drawer."

So, these writers pull down an indie-published story, give up on a story, usually out of fear, and put the story in a drawer. No reader will ever buy it.

Headshaking in this modern world of unlimited shelf space.

So this rule (in this new world) means get the story available to readers and leave it there.

Giving Up

The new world of indie publishing also causes another major problem with this rule that I see and hear about all the time.

It goes like this for short stories:

Writer: I've tried the short story at three markets. I'm going to indie publish it now.

Me: (Thinking) *Dumb.*

I never say that to any writer with my out-loud voice. But I think it.

For a short story, the advantages of selling to major magazines or top anthologies is far, far greater in both money and exposure and free advertising.

Sure, at some point you don't want to go below a 5-cent-per-word market, but wow are there a lot of that level markets out there.

It goes like this for novels:

Writer: I've tried the novel at three agents for two years and rewritten it twice for agents. I'm going to indie publish it now.

Me: (Thinking) *Dumb that you sent the novel there in the first place. You wasted all those years never putting it on the market.*

I never say that to any writer with my out-loud voice. But I think it.

Oh, wow, do I think it.

Agents are not a market.

So the new world of indie publishing is causing, with Rule #5, writers to stay up on the business, to find top short-fiction markets, to watch what is happening with the major book publishers, and to learn how to indie publish their own work.

That is all good, if you do it.

Boiling Rule #5 Down

Simple. Keep the story or novel on the market until it sells. For short stories, keep it going to the top short-fiction magazines. For novels, get it indie published and then leave it alone for a few years.

And if you have to touch it after a few years, do a better cover, learn how to write better blurbs, and make sure your formatting is working on all devices.

But past that, leave it alone.

Don't rewrite the story or novel because some reviewer said something. (Really the dumbest thing I have heard in this new world.)

Don't give up on the short story just because it has a few rejections.

Don't pull a story down from indie published because it only sold a few copies in a year.

Rule #5: You must keep it on the market.

For writers who have made it this far in the writing process, not following this rule will often swallow their work in self-doubt and wasted time.

Follow the rule. It's a simple rule.

Don't waste the time.

EPILOGUE

Robert A. Heinlein called these five rules "Business Habits." I couldn't agree more.

Even though the first three talk about writing, they are firmly in how a writer manages his or her own business.

As Heinlein said, talking about the five business habits:

"… they are amazingly hard to follow—which is why there are so few professional writers and so many aspirants, and which is why I am not afraid to give away the racket!"

After following these rules since 1982 and making a living with my fiction writing since 1987, I can attest to how hard these five simple rules are to follow.

I would fall off, my writing would grind to a halt, I would realize I had slipped, and I would get back onto the rules.

Don't be mad at yourself when you slip off these rules if you really want to follow them.

Just keep going at it.

A Few Additions That Need to be Made

First, you can follow the above rules like a perfect clock and they will do you no good if you don't continue to learn how to be a better storyteller.

Learning is critical because the business rules are guidelines to practice.

Learn, then practice, then learn, then practice.

Learning how to be a better storyteller is critical to making these rules work for you.

And that learning never stops. Ever.

Second, there is no place in the five business rules that Heinlein talks about speed of typing or production or all the other favorite topics writers have these days.

You can follow these rules just fine if you only have ten minutes a day to write or if you have ten hours.

However, Heinlein's Rules, if followed, will allow you to have far more fun with your writing, something I hear that many writers have lost lately.

Third, you must keep up with the business side of the industry. Heinlein called these his "Business Habits." You need to also make it a habit to understand the new world of publishing and follow the changes.

The advice I gave above is for 2016, the year this book was published.

I have no idea if the indie world will look the same in 2018, or if traditional book publishing will collapse or start giving writers their real value and decent contracts.

But whatever happens, follow the publishing business, stay up with it as best you can.

I hope these five business rules from the great Robert A. Heinlein will help you with your own writing going forward.

I know I owe my entire career to them.

And I still follow them.

Have fun with your writing.

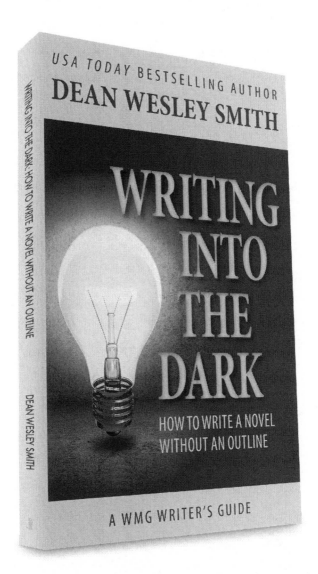

USA TODAY BESTSELLING AUTHOR
DEAN WESLEY SMITH

WRITING INTO THE DARK

HOW TO WRITE A NOVEL WITHOUT AN OUTLINE

A WMG WRITER'S GUIDE

If you enjoyed *Heinlein's Rules,* you might
also enjoy *Writing into the Dark,* available now
from your favorite bookseller.

Turn the page for a sample.

CHAPTER ONE

SOME BACKGROUND

The reason there are very few articles or books about writing into the dark is because the process gets such horrid bad press. Just the idea of writing without planning ahead on a project as long as a novel makes most English professors shudder and shake their head and turn away in disgust.

And beginning writers mostly just can't imagine doing that. It just seems impossible.

Yet, many long-term professional writers write this way. And many of the books those same English professors study were written completely into the dark.

So why do all of us, as we are growing up, buy into the idea that novels must be outlined to the last little detail to work?

First, the problem comes from the fact that we all started out as readers.

To readers, writers know it all. They know enough to make that plot twist work, that foreshadowing inserted at just the right place, the gun planted when it needs to be planted to be fired later, and so on.

To readers, writers are really smart to be able to do all that.

Then we get into school and all the English teachers build on that belief system by taking apart books and talking about the deep meaning and what the writer was doing. And that makes writers seem even smarter and the process of writing a novel even more daunting.

So the desire to outline is logical, totally logical, after all that.

In fact, it seems like outlining is the only way to do a complex novel.

But interestingly enough, that very process of outlining often kills the very complex structure the writer is hoping to achieve.

A HUMBLING EXPERIENCE

Two of the most humbling experiences in my life occurred the two times I went into a graduate-level English class at a university as a professional writer. (Do not do this if you can avoid it.)

The first time, the English professor, doing his job, had the students read and discuss two of my short stories BEFORE I GOT THERE.

So two of my stories were deconstructed by fifteen graduate English department students.

So I arrived, talked some about what it was like to be a freelance fiction writer, and then the professor turned the discussion to my two stories they had read. And I started to get questions about how did I know to put in the second hidden meaning of the story, or the foreshadowing of an upcoming event, or...or...or...

They all knew far, far more about those two stories than I did.

Honestly, I could barely remember the stories, and I had no idea I had even put in all that extra stuff they were all so impressed by.

And the reason I couldn't remember is that my subconscious, my creative brain, put all that in. My critical, conscious brain had nothing at all to do with it.

I had just let my creative brain tell a story.

Nothing more.

The problem was that for weeks after that first time into that class, I couldn't get all that crap back out of my head. I found myself wondering about second meanings, about subplots, about foreshadowing—all those other English-class terms. Froze me down completely until I got past it.

Let me be clear here. My critical brain is not smart enough to put all that stuff in. Luckily for me, my creative brain seems to be smart enough if I get my critical brain out of the way and let it.

But getting that stupid critical brain out of the way is the key problem.

BREAKING OUT OF THE TAUGHT PROBLEM

All of us go into writing novels with all that training of thinking we need to know all that stuff about subplots, foreshadowing, sub-meanings, and so on. Thinking about it, I find it amazing that with the training we get, any novel gets written at all.

Or that any writer even gets started writing.

And outlining seems to be the logical process when faced with all that. In fact, outlining would be the only way to let the critical brain even pretend to be smart.

When I started writing solidly, novels seemed flat impossible. I could manage a short story in an afternoon, but anything beyond that was a concrete wall of paralyzing fear.

So how did I break out of the problem of everything I had been taught?

I used to own a bookstore. One fine slow afternoon, I was sitting in the front room of my bookstore and I looked around at all the books in the room. And I had a realization that in hindsight sounds damn silly.

I realized that people, regular people, wrote all those books.

And what all those regular people did was just sit down and tell a story.

They were entertainers.

That simple.

It was no magic process that only really special English-department-anointed people could do. And if all those regular people with all those books covering the walls of my bookstore could do it, then I could do it as well.

So I looked at how I felt writing short stories.

At that point I just wrote a story and stopped when the story was over. Nothing more fancy. I figured I could do that with a novel as well.

So after that realization, over the next few years I started five or six novels and got stuck at the one-third point where I could no longer fight the critical voice into submission. I had no tools to fight the critical voice at that point in time, to be honest.

So two years after that realization, mad at myself for not finishing a novel and for making novels into something "important" instead of just fun, entertaining stories, I sat down at my trusty typewriter and thought only about writing ten pages a day.

I had no outline, nothing. My focus was on finishing ten pages. Period.

Thirty days later I had finished an 80,000-word novel.

My first written novel.

The next day, I started into a second novel, doing ten pages a day again.

I powered my way through the need, the belief, the fear of doing a novel the way it "should" be done.

And never ever had that fear again. I had other fears, sure, but not that one.

Every long-term novel writer has some story of getting past the need for major outlines, for major planning. A lot of younger professionals are still banging out outlines and following them.

Again, no right way.

But eventually, if you are going to be around for a long time and writing, you need to feed the reader part of your brain and just write for fun.

Otherwise, knowing the ending of a novel, having it all figured out ahead of time, is just too dull and boring and way too much work.

To read more, pick up a copy of *Writing into the Dark* from your favorite retailer.

Be the first to know!

Just sign up for the Dean Wesley Smith newsletter, and keep up with the latest news, releases and so much more—even the occasional giveaway.

To sign up, go to deanwesleysmith.com.

But wait! There's more. Sign up for the WMG Publishing newsletter, too, and get the latest news and releases from all of the WMG authors and lines, including Kristine Kathryn Rusch, Kristine Grayson, Kris Nelscott, *Fiction River: An Original Anthology Magazine, Smith's Monthly,* and so much more.

Just go to wmgpublishing.com and click on Newsletter.

More Books by
Dean Wesley Smith

Stages of a Fiction Writer:
Know Where You Stand on the Path to Writing

Writing into the Dark:
How to Write a Novel without an Outline

Killing the Top Ten Sacred Cows of Indie Publishing

How to Write a Novel in Ten Days

Killing the Top Ten Sacred Cows of Publishing

Think Like a Publisher: A Step-By-Step Guide
to Publishing Your Own Books

More Books by
Dean Wesley Smith

Stages of a Fiction Writer:
Know Where You Stand on the Path to Writing

Writing into the Dark:
How to Write a Novel without an Outline

Killing the Top Ten Sacred Cows of Indie Publishing

How to Write a Novel in Ten Days

Killing the Top Ten Sacred Cows of Publishing

Think Like a Publisher: A Step-By-Step Guide
to Publishing Your Own Books

ABOUT THE AUTHOR

USA Today bestselling writer Dean Wesley Smith published more than a hundred novels in thirty years and hundreds of short stories across many genres.

He wrote a couple dozen *Star Trek* novels, the only two original *Men in Black* novels, Spider-Man and X-Men novels, plus novels set in gaming and television worlds. He wrote novels under dozens of pen names in the worlds of comic books and movies, including novelizations of a dozen films, from *The Final Fantasy* to *Steel* to *Rundown*.

He now writes his own original fiction under just the one name, Dean Wesley Smith. In addition to his upcoming novel releases, his monthly magazine called *Smith's Monthly* premiered October 1, 2013, filled entirely with his original novels and stories.

Dean also worked as an editor and publisher, first at Pulphouse Publishing, then for *VB Tech Journal,* then for Pocket Books. He now plays a role as an executive editor for the original anthology series *Fiction River.*

For more information go to www.deanwesleysmith.com, www.smithsmonthly.com or www.fictionriver.com.

Made in the USA
San Bernardino, CA
08 March 2018